PIMP MY NOODLES

PIMP MY NOODLES

Turn Instant Noodles & Ramen Into Fabulous Feasts!

Kathy Kordalis

hardie grant books

Contents

Introduction

Welcome to the world of noodles! Noodles are endlessly versatile, so quick and easy to prepare. All you need to do is add some protein and vegetables for a complete and nutritious meal. Opt for cheap and cheerful for easy mid-week suppers, or more elegant dishes to feed a crowd; wow your friends with authentic flavour combinations or plan meals in advance to save time. Reinvent and update existing recipes with a few pimping tips and make the most out of your well-chosen essential ingredients. For optional extras, refer to the Shopping List on page 16; these are just a few fridge, freezer and cupboard essentials that you can use every day to jazz up your dishes.

Find different ways to cook eggs in the Pimping chapter; recipes to Energise you for busy weeks; meals to help you Restore & Recover from the morning after the night before; Party dishes for entertaining or to feed a crowd; Cold Noodle Plates for quick and easy lunches; and Survival dishes for mid-week meals. You'll also discover One-Pot wonders and noodle bowls to keep you nourished.

THE
ESSENTIALS

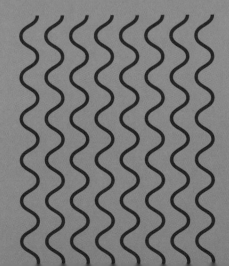

Types of Noodles

In Asia, noodles can be found in dishes everywhere – from street food vendors to the tables of celebration feasts. Noodle dishes – symbolic of happiness, health, friendship, and commitment – are important at nearly every meal. Although they are generally associated with Asian cuisine, they also fare well with more continental flavours. What we know as pasta today was, in fact, introduced to Italy after Marco Polo travelled to China. There are many types of noodles to choose from, but below is a good selection that are readily available in most supermarkets:

Instant noodles

These are dried, pre-cooked noodle blocks that come with a flavoured powder such as chicken or vegetable. They are either cooked or soaked in boiling water before eating, and are quick and easy to prepare – a perfect one-pot meal.

Rice noodles

These are made from ground rice and water and come in many widths, ranging from vermicelli to flat ribbon noodles. They are best served once soaked or boiled in water and are a great vehicle for sauces.

Bean or cellophane thread noodles

These noodles, also known as glass noodles, are a type of transparent noodle made from starch and are most commonly sold as very fine strands in bundles. The starch can come from sweet potato or mung beans. All these need is a good soak in boiling water. They work very well in salads.

Egg noodles

These are egg-enriched wheat noodles and are commonly used in Chinese cuisine. They come in a variety of thicknesses and need to be cooked in boiling water until soft before use. They are a little more robust than other noodles so are great in a stir-fry.

Udon noodles

Udon noodles are the thickest type of Japanese noodle, made from wheat flour, salt and water. These noodles are most commonly served in a broth, usually flavoured with mirin and soy sauce.

Ramen noodles

These are used in Japanese cuisine and are made with egg, flour and salt. There are many varieties of ramen noodle, from wavy to straight, thin to thick, and just as many variations of broth. They are very versatile and can be used in soups and stir-fries. In fact, I have used them in this book to make ramen noodle buns for a burger (see page 74)!

Soba noodles

Soba noodles hail from Japan. Made from buckwheat flour, they have a nutty flavour and a slightly chewy texture and are great in salads.

Vegetable noodles

Courgetti or courgette (zucchini) noodles are thin strands of spiralized courgette. You can also spiralize butternut squash (pumpkin), beetroot (beet), sweet potato and many more vegetables. These are best served raw or flash cooked as a substitute or addition to ordinary noodles.

Shopping List

Cupboard

Spices, sauces, pastes, oils, vinegars and powdered stock are just a few essentials that help to build flavour and pimp your dishes. Here are a few suggestions:

baked beans	peanut butter
chilli flakes	rice wine vinegar
chilli paste	sea salt
cinnamon	sesame oil
condensed milk	soy sauce
five spice	sun-dried tomato paste
ginger paste	sweet chilli sauce
honey	tahini
hot chilli sauce	tomato purée (paste)
miso	vegetable stock powder
Nutella®	wasabi

Freezer

Fresh is best but if you lead a busy life, you may not always have the time to get to the shops, so keep a well-stocked freezer with essentials to pimp your noodles in an instant.

Frozen mixed vegetables: such as green beans, cauliflower, carrots and peas. A perfect way to add a quick nutritious boost to your mid-week meal.

Frozen berries: these are a brilliant way to make a quick dessert.

Frozen herbs: great to have when you can't make it to the shops or the months aren't sunny enough to maintain your own herb garden.

Frozen natural flavourings: such as garlic, ginger and chopped onions.

Frozen lemon and lime juice: in ice cube trays.

Frozen stock: for broths and soups.

Frozen grated cheese: a brilliant time saver.

Frozen butter: in portions ready to be added to sauces.

A few freezing tips

Your freezer is your friend. Follow these simple tips to get the most out of it.

Cool foods before you freeze them.

Wrap foods properly or put them in sealed containers, otherwise your food can get freezer burn.

If in doubt, throw it out. If you are unsure how long something has been frozen, don't take any chances.

Fridge

You can use any of the following fridge staples to whip up a great pimped noodle dish:

bacon

butter

coriander (cilantro)

crème fraîche

eggs

grated Cheddar

ham

limes and lemons

mayonnaise

Parmesan

parsley

rocket (arugula) or spinach

rosemary

thyme

tofu

PIMPING

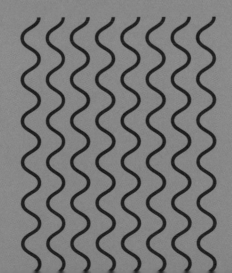

You can pimp your noodles by using condiments; add peanut butter or Nutella®, some vegetables, protein or tofu, quick broths... and best of all, eggs! If you're feeling lazy, topping your noodles with a fried or poached egg is an easy, instant way to shake things up. Similarly, you could boil and chop an egg and scatter over your noodles for something a little different.

Fried eggs

A deliciously indulgent addition to your noodles.

In a frying pan over a medium-low heat, add 1 tablespoon olive oil. Crack the eggs into the pan. When they're ready, remove the pan from the heat and use a spatula to take the eggs out. Delicious on top of noodles.

Poached eggs

Poached eggs give a great protein boost to any dish.

On the hob: make sure your eggs are really fresh – the fresher the egg, the tighter the poach. In order to help the whites coagulate quicker, add a small dash of vinegar to a pan of steadily simmering water. Crack the egg into a small bowl. Using a whisk, swirl the water to create a gentle whirlpool to help the egg white wrap around the yolk. Slowly tip the egg into the water, and cook for 3–4 minutes. You want to achieve a firm white, and gooey but still runny yolk. Remove the egg using a slotted spoon and drain on paper towels before you serve.

In the microwave: gently crack an egg into a suitable container filled with water, making sure it's completely submerged. Cover with a saucer and microwave on high for about 1 minute, or until the white is set but the yolk is still runny. Use a slotted spoon to transfer the egg to a plate.

Boiled eggs

Serve boiled eggs halved or chopped on top of a bowl of noodles of your choice.

For the runny 5-minute egg, bring a saucepan of water to the boil and gently drop in room-temperature eggs. Put the timer on for 5 minutes, then carefully remove the eggs. Run them under cold water and peel.

For the almost set 7-minute egg, bring a saucepan of water to the boil and gently drop in room-temperature eggs. Put the timer on for 7 minutes, then carefully remove the eggs. Run them under cold water and peel.

For the set-yet-creamy 9-minute egg, bring a saucepan of water to the boil and gently drop in room-temperature eggs. Put the timer on for 9 minutes, then carefully remove the eggs. Run them under cold water and peel.

Soy Eggs (inspired by Momofuku)

2 large eggs, at room temperature

1 tsp caster (superfine) sugar

1 tbsp apple cider vinegar

30 ml (1 fl oz) soy sauce

salt and freshly ground black pepper

These delicately flavoured eggs were inspired by Momofuku noodle bar in New York.

Bring a saucepan of water to the boil and gently drop in the eggs. Put the timer on for 7 minutes, then carefully remove the eggs. Run them under cold water and peel.

Meanwhile, in a bowl, mix the sugar, apple cider vinegar and soy sauce, then add the eggs. For the best result, marinate overnight or for a minimum of 1 hour. Serve seasoned with salt and pepper.

Omelette

1–2 tbsp unsalted butter

3 medium eggs, beaten

fillings of choice

Noodles and omelette – the perfect pairing.

Gently heat the butter in a small frying pan. Add the egg mixture and tilt the pan so the mixture covers the base. As the omelette sets, use a heatproof plastic spatula or flat-edged wooden spoon to gently lift and stir, tilting the pan so the uncooked egg runs underneath. Cook for 1–2 minutes or until golden and just set underneath. The top should still be slightly runny – it will continue to cook after you fill and fold the omelette.

Add your fillings of choice, lift one side of the omelette and fold it over to enclose the filling. Carefully slide onto a serving plate, slice and serve immediately.

Quick Kimchi

Makes 1 jar

1 tsp salt

½ Chinese cabbage, torn

2 garlic cloves, finely chopped

1 tsp caster (superfine) sugar

1 tbsp chilli powder

3 tbsp fish sauce

4 spring onions (scallions), cut into 3 cm (1 in) lengths

1 tbsp sesame oil

pinch of mixed sesame seeds

This is a quick and fresher version of the classic recipe.

Scatter the salt over the cabbage leaves and set aside in a large bowl for 5 minutes. In a small bowl, combine the garlic, sugar, chilli powder and fish sauce to form a paste.

Add the spring onions, sesame oil and seeds, and chilli paste to the cabbage. Using your hands, rub the chilli paste into the other ingredients until well combined. Store in an airtight container. It will keep refrigerated for 1 week.

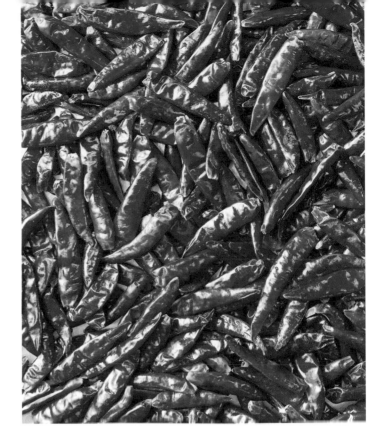

Quick Chilli Lime Sauce

Makes 1 portion

2 garlic cloves, crushed

2 fresh chillies, finely chopped

2 tsp caster (superfine) sugar

60 ml (2 fl oz) lime juice

2 tbsp fish sauce

4 kaffir lime leaves, sliced into thin strips (optional)

Top a cold noodle dish with this dressing, adding some bamboo shoots, coriander (cilantro) and spring onions (scallions).

In a pestle and mortar, grind the garlic and chillies into a paste. Add the sugar, lime juice and fish sauce. Stir everything together and taste. Add the lime leaves, if using.

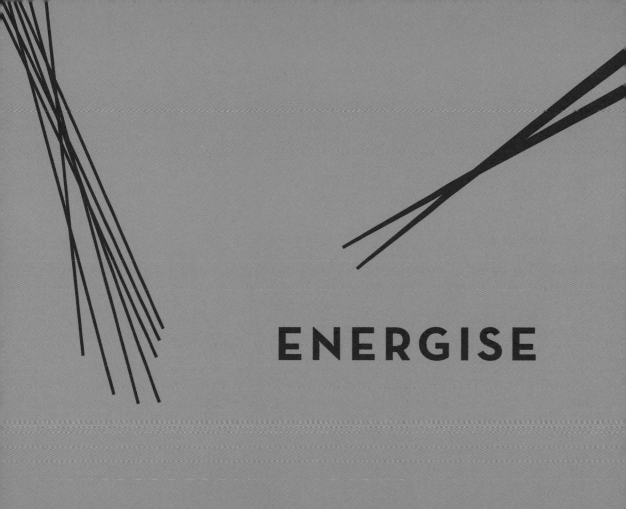

ENERGISE

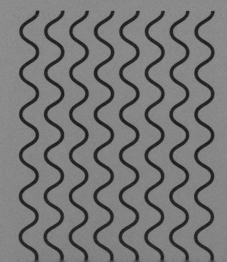

Bang Bang Chicken

Serves 2

150 g (5 oz) thin egg noodles, cooked according to the packet instructions

2 cooked chicken breast fillets

½ cucumber, deseeded and cut into long, thin strips (replicating noodles)

1 carrot, cut into long, thin strips (replicating noodles)

1 small red (bell) pepper, cut into matchsticks

3 spring onions (scallions), thinly sliced diagonally

100 g (3½ oz) beansprouts

Sichuan dressing:

1 tsp Sichuan peppercorns

2 tbsp soy sauce

2 tbsp rice wine vinegar

1 tbsp honey

1 tbsp Sriracha

1 red Thai chilli, halved lengthways

This feisty salad is light and fresh and will keep you energised. It's based on a traditional Chinese street food dish and is enhanced by Sriracha, Sichuan peppercorns and rice wine vinegar, which are readily available in most supermarkets.

Start by making the dressing. Use a pestle and mortar to crush the peppercorns. Place them in a bowl with the other ingredients and mix well.

For the noodles, shred the chicken and place it in a bowl with half the dressing. Add the cucumber, carrot, pepper, spring onions, beansprouts and dressing to the noodles. Toss to combine, then pour over the rest of the dressing. Divide between 2 bowls and serve.

Crispy Noodle Meatballs

Makes 16 meatballs – enough for 2 or 3 people

100 g (3½ oz) thin egg noodles, cooked according to the packet instructions

2 tbsp lemongrass paste

1 garlic clove, crushed

3 cm (1 in) piece ginger, peeled and grated, or 2 tbsp ginger paste

300 g (10½ oz) pork mince (ground pork)

1 tbsp fish sauce

1 tbsp soy sauce

1 tbsp sesame oil

2 spring onions (scallions), thinly sliced

½ small bunch coriander (cilantro) leaves, chopped

vegetable oil, for frying

steamed pak choi, to serve

sweet chilli sauce, to serve

lime wedges, to serve

The combination of the lemongrass, seasoning and crispy noodles make these meatballs irresistible. A perfect make-ahead meal.

Combine the noodles, lemongrass paste, garlic, ginger, pork, fish sauce, soy sauce, sesame oil, spring onions and coriander in a bowl. Mix well.

Using wet hands, roll heaped tablespoonfuls of the mixture into balls. Heat around 2 cm (¾ in) oil in a wok over medium-high heat. Cook the meatballs in batches, turning them often, for 7–10 minutes or until golden. Reheat the oil between batches. Using a slotted spoon, remove the meatballs.

Serve the meatballs with steamed pak choi, sweet chilli sauce and lime wedges.

Miso & Tofu
Udon Noodles

~~~~~~~~~~~~

Serves 2

200 g (7 oz) udon noodles, cooked according to the packet instructions

4 tbsp white miso paste

2 handfuls of baby spinach

200 g (7 oz) tofu, cubed

100 g (3½ oz) button mushrooms, sliced

Soothing and nutritious – a perfect warming meal.

Combine the miso and 500 ml (17 fl oz) cold water in a large saucepan over a medium-high heat. Cook, stirring, for 2 minutes or until the paste has dissolved. Cover. Gently simmer so as not to kill any of the goodness of the miso paste.

Add the spinach leaves, tofu and mushrooms to the miso mixture. Cook for 2 minutes or until the leaves have just wilted. Divide the noodles between the bowls. Ladle over the miso mixture. Serve.

Quick Pho

Serves 2

200 g (7 oz) flat noodles, cooked according to the packet instructions

500 ml (17 fl oz) beef stock

2 thick slices ginger, peeled

1 onion, thinly sliced

2 garlic cloves, sliced

3 star anise

1 cinnamon stick, lightly bruised

1 tbsp caster (superfine) sugar

2 tbsp fish sauce

200 g (7 oz) beef steak such as sirloin, thinly sliced

20 g (¾ oz) beansprouts

1 long red chilli, deseeded and thinly sliced, to serve

½ bunch coriander (cilantro), leaves picked, to serve

lime wedges, to serve

This cheat is a great way to recreate the flavours that usually take hours to develop in a broth.

Add the stock to a saucepan along with the ginger, onion, garlic, star anise, cinnamon, sugar and fish sauce. Bring to the boil, then reduce the heat to low. Cover and simmer for 20 minutes. Strain, then return the soup to the pan. Cover and return to the boil.

Divide the noodles among warmed soup bowls, then top with the sliced beef steak. Pour over the hot soup mixture (the heat will gently cook the meat) and top with the beansprouts. Serve garnished with chilli, coriander and lime wedges.

Veg & Noodle Omelette

Serves 1

100 g (3½ oz) egg noodles, cooked according to the packet instructions

3 medium eggs

salt and freshly ground black pepper

2 tbsp vegetable oil

½ pack prepared stirfry vegetable mix (approx 100g/3½ oz)

2 cm (¾ in) piece fresh ginger, peeled and finely grated, or 2 tsp ginger paste

1 tbsp oyster sauce

2 tsp sesame oil

2 spring onions (scallions), finely chopped

Sriracha and crushed Sichuan peppercorns, to serve

A quick and healthy start or end to the day.

Whisk the eggs with salt and pepper in a bowl and set aside.

Place a 20 cm (8 in) frying pan (skillet) over a high heat. Add 1 tablespoon oil, swirling the pan to coat it. Add the vegetable mix, ginger, oyster sauce and sesame oil. Stir-fry for 2–3 minutes or until the vegetables are just tender, and top with the spring onions. Transfer to a bowl. Add the noodles and toss to combine.

Heat the remaining vegetable oil in the same pan over a medium heat. Add the eggs and move the pan around to spread them out evenly. Cook for 30 seconds or until just set.

Top one half of omelette with the vegetable mixture. Cook for 1–2 minutes or until the egg has set. Fold the omelette over to enclose the filling. Slide onto a plate. Cover to keep warm. Pimp with a drizzle of Sriracha and some crushed Sichuan peppercorns.

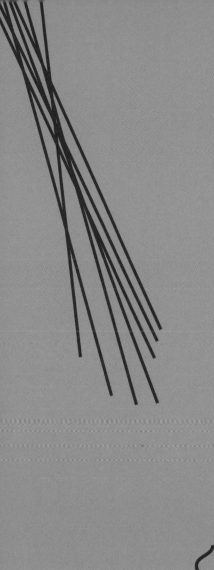

COLD
NOODLE
PLATES

Soba & Tuna Noodles

Serves 2

150 g (5 oz) dried soba noodles, cooked according to the packet instructions

120 g (4 oz) tinned tuna in olive oil, drained weight

100 g (3½ oz) tomatoes, halved

1 medium avocado, chopped

big handful of mixed herbs, chopped

juice of ½ lemon

1 tbsp rice wine vinegar

1 tbsp soy sauce

½ tbsp honey

1 tbsp mixed sesame seeds

salt and freshly ground black pepper

2 spring onions (scallions), sliced, to serve

A perfect, quick, wholesome salad that keeps well. Make a batch ahead for packed lunches.

Drain the tuna, reserving 2 tablespoons oil. Place the tuna in a large bowl, then flake with a fork. Add the noodles, tomatoes, avocado and herbs.

Place the reserved oil, lemon juice, rice wine vinegar, soy sauce, honey and sesame seeds in a jug and mix well. Season with salt and pepper. Add to the mixture, toss to combine and serve topped with the spring onions.

Kale & Noodle Goodness Bowl with Poached Eggs

Serves 2

100g (3½ oz) sesame noodles, cooked according to the packet instructions

dash of vinegar

2 very fresh medium eggs

100 g (3½ oz) tinned beluga lentils, drained and rinsed

30 g (1 oz) kale, blanched

60 g (2 oz) tenderstem broccoli, blanched

60 g (2 oz) red cabbage, thinly sliced

100 g (3½ oz) butternut squash, roasted and thinly sliced

1 avocado, thinly sliced

sesame seeds, to serve

Dressing:

3 tbsp tahini

juice of ½ lemon

3-4 tbsp warm water

Jam-packed with goodness, this combo can be pre-made and topped with the poached eggs when you are ready to go. For a more substantial meal, add some shredded poached chicken.

To make the dressing, combine all of the ingredients, adding a little more water if necessary, until it is a thick but pourable liquid.

Add a small dash of vinegar to a pan of steadily simmering water. Crack the eggs individually into a ramekin or cup. Using a whisk, create a gentle whirlpool in the water to help the egg white wrap around the yolk. Slowly tip the first egg into the water. Cook for 3 minutes. Remove with a slotted spoon, cutting off any wispy edges using the edge of the spoon. Drain on kitchen paper. Repeat with the second egg.

On 2 plates, arrange the lentils, all of the prepared vegetables, the noodles and the poached eggs, then drizzle with the dressing and sprinkle with sesame seeds.

Duck Papaya Salad

Serves 2

100 g (3½ oz) soba noodles, cooked according to the packet instructions

100 g (3½ oz) smoked duck, sliced

100 g (3½ oz) green beans, blanched

½ ripe papaya, scooped

100 g (3½ oz) cherry tomatoes, quartered

1–2 small red chillies, deseeded and finely chopped (depending how hot you like it)

handful of mint leaves, torn

handful of coriander (cilantro) leaves, torn

handful of Thai basil leaves, torn

Quick Thai dressing:

½ tbsp fish sauce

1 tbsp sweet chilli sauce

1 tbsp lime juice

This is a take on the Thai green papaya salad. The ripe papaya adds a buttery, sweet and musky element – perfect with the duck and sharp dressing.

To make the quick Thai dressing, mix all the ingredients together in a small bowl.

In a large bowl, mix the noodles, duck, green beans, papaya, cherry tomatoes, chillies, mint leaves, coriander and Thai basil.

Top with the quick Thai dressing and serve in bowls.

Nuoc Cham Vermicelli Salad

Serves 2

125 g (4 oz) dried rice vermicelli noodles, cooked according to the packet instructions

4 chicken thighs (skin on)

1 tbsp rapeseed oil

1 large carrot, thinly sliced using a mandolin

1 cucumber, halved lengthways, thinly sliced into half moons

handful of mint leaves, torn

handful of coriander (cilantro) leaves, torn

60 g (2 oz) bean sprouts (optional)

lime wedges and chilli sauce, to serve

Nuoc cham dressing:

2 tbsp palm sugar (or granulated/raw sugar)

2 tbsp fish sauce

juice of 1½ limes

1 long red chilli, deseeded and finely chopped

2 crushed garlic cloves

3 cm (1 in) piece ginger, peeled and finely grated

This nuoc cham dressing is super versatile; I recommend making a batch and keeping it in the fridge. This salad also works well with leftover roast beef.

Preheat the oven to 180°C (350°F/Gas 4). Drizzle the oil into a baking tray and roast the chicken thighs for 30–40 minutes or until cooked through.

Meanwhile, combine all of the nuoc cham dressing ingredients in a large jug. Stir until the sugar dissolves. Using kitchen scissors, cut the noodles into 5 cm (2 in) lengths and place into a large bowl.

Add the remaining ingredients and the roasted chicken thighs, then pour over the dressing. Toss gently to combine. Serve with lime wedges and chilli sauce for a little kick.

Udon Noodle Salad

Serves 2

100 g (3½ oz) udon noodles, cooked according to the packet instructions

1 × 3-egg omelette (see p 28), rolled up and thinly sliced

100 g (3½ oz) ham, shredded

60 g (2 oz) radishes, chopped

60 g (2 oz) green beans, blanched

2 handfuls of baby spinach

10 g (½ oz) hijiki sea vegetables, rehydrated

2 spring onions (scallions), sliced

pinch of furikake (Japanese seasoning)

Miso wasabi dressing:

1 tbsp white miso

1 tsp wasabi

1 tbsp rice vinegar

juice of ½ lime

1–2 tbsp warm water, to taste

This Japanese-inspired salad is another perfect lunch-box meal.

Make the dressing by mixing together the miso, wasabi, rice vinegar, lime juice and water, if needed, and set aside.

On 2 plates, arrange the noodles, omelette, ham, radishes, green beans, spinach, hijiki and spring onions. Top with the dressing and finish with the furikake.

Korean Wonder Pots

~~~~~~~~~~

Serves 2

100 g (3½ oz) sesame noodles, cooked according to the packet instructions

½ cucumber, thinly sliced

2 spring onions (scallions), thinly sliced

1 raw beetroot (beet), peeled and grated

4 radishes, thinly sliced

60 g (2 oz) Quick Kimchi (see p 30)

2 tbsp gochujang

2 tbsp soy sauce

100 g (3½ oz) sirloin steak, cooked and thinly sliced

1 × 7-minute egg (see p 26), halved

200 ml (7 fl oz) vegetable stock, to serve (optional)

These pots are inspired by the Korean dish naengmyeon, which consists of noodles served cold in a broth. Eat them cold, as is traditional, for a new sensation, or hot, as you prefer. The addition of gochujang, a sweet, spicy, salty Korean condiment made from red chillies, fermented soybeans and glutinous rice, brings a depth of flavour. Kimchi, a traditional dish of fermented vegetables, is proven to have outstanding nutritional benefits.

Place the noodles, cucumber, spring onions, beetroot, radishes, kimchi, gochujang, soy sauce, steak and egg in 2 glass jars and seal them so you can take them wherever you want to go. They can be kept in the fridge for 2–3 days.

Pour the stock into the jar, or use just-boiled water if you prefer, and allow to sit for 3 minutes before serving. This dish is usually eaten cold in Korea, but lukewarm is fine too.

Miso Salmon, Ribbon-cut Vegetables & Cellophane Noodles

Serves 2

50 g (2 oz) cellophane or rice vermicelli noodles, cooked according to the packet instructions

2 tsp white miso paste

2 tsp mirin

1 tsp soy sauce

1 tsp sesame oil

2 salmon fillets

100 g (3½ oz) ribbon-cut vegetables

2 spring onions (scallions), thinly sliced

1 tsp sesame seeds

handful of fresh coriander (cilantro), to serve

Miso ginger dressing:

4 tbsp mirin

2 tbsp soy sauce

1 tbsp rice vinegar

1 tbsp freshly grated ginger

1 tsp sesame oil

2 tsp white miso paste

A quick and easy dish that doesn't skimp on flavour!

Combine the miso, mirin, soy sauce and sesame oil in a small bowl. Coat the salmon in the marinade and set aside for 15 minutes.

To make the dressing, combine the mirin, soy sauce, rice vinegar, ginger and sesame oil in a small saucepan and bring to a simmer. Remove from the heat, add the miso paste, stir until combined and allow to cool.

Preheat the grill (broiler) to high. Grill (broil) the salmon for 3 minutes until golden and cooked most of the way through.

Meanwhile, in a bowl, mix the noodles, ribbon-cut vegetables and spring onions with half the dressing. Mix well and place onto 2 plates. Top each salad with a piece of salmon and finish with the sesame seeds, the remaining dressing and coriander.

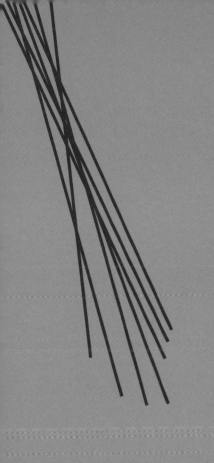

RESTORE & RECOVER

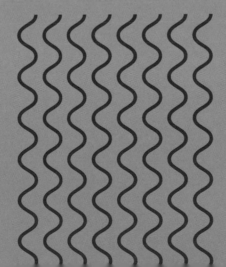

Chicken Fried Noodles

Serves 2

200 g (7 oz) thin egg noodles, cooked according to the packet instructions

2 tbsp oyster sauce

2 tbsp soy sauce

1 tsp Sriracha

300 g (10½ oz) chicken breast fillets, cut into thin strips

2 tsp Chinese five-spice powder

2 tbsp rapeseed oil

1 orange (bell) pepper, seeds removed, thinly sliced

2 spring onions (scallions), roughly chopped

2 garlic cloves, crushed

1 tbsp ginger paste

100 g (3½ oz) mangetout (snow peas), trimmed

100 g (3½ oz) mushrooms, sliced

75 g (2½ oz) cashews, to serve

A retro classic that never disappoints!

Place the oyster sauce, soy sauce and Sriracha into a bowl, stir to combine, then set aside.

Meanwhile, rub the chicken with the five-spice powder. Place 1 tablespoon oil in a wok over a high heat, add the chicken and cook until golden.

Add the remaining oil to the wok and stir-fry the pepper for 1–2 minutes. Add the spring onions, garlic, ginger, mangetout and mushrooms and stir-fry for another minute. Return the chicken to the pan, add the reserved sauce and cook for 1 minute until thickened.

Add the noodles and cashews and serve.

Beef & Black Bean Sauce

~~~~~~~~~~~~~~~

Serves 2

Crispy noodle base:

150 g (5 oz) egg noodles, cooked according to the packet instructions

2 tsp sesame oil, plus extra for greasing

pinch of salt

Beef and black bean sauce:

2 tbsp vegetable oil

1 onion, sliced

2 garlic cloves, sliced

1 tbsp ginger paste

1 green (bell) pepper, roughly chopped

300 g (10½ oz) beef strips

3–4 tbsp black bean sauce

2 spring onions (scallions), cut diagonally

drizzle of honey

squeeze of Sriracha

This crispy noodle and savoury meaty sauce combo is a winner!

Preheat the oven to 180°C (350°F/Gas 4). Toss the noodles with 1 teaspoon sesame oil.

Grease a 20 cm (8 in) square baking dish with a little oil. Add the noodles and remaining sesame oil, sprinkle with salt and bake for 10 minutes. Check that the noodles are cooking evenly, then bake for a further 5 minutes or until crisp and golden.

For the beef and black bean sauce, heat 1 teaspoon oil in a frying pan (skillet) over a medium-high heat. Add the onion, garlic, ginger and pepper and stir-fry for 5 minutes. Add the beef and cook for a further 5 minutes, then add the black bean sauce, spring onions, honey and Sriracha and cook for a further 5 minutes. Serve on top of the crispy noodles.

Pad Thai

Serves 2

150 g (5 oz) Thai flat-rice noodles, cooked according to the packet instructions

2 tbsp vegetable oil

1 onion, sliced

100 g (3½ oz) tofu, drained and cubed

4 tbsp pad Thai paste or more to taste

265 g (9½ oz) ribbon-cut stir-fry vegetable mix

50 g (2 oz) peanuts, chopped, to serve

2 tsp chilli flakes, to serve

lime wedges, to serve

If you like, you can pimp this classic dish with some strips of omelette and serve with lime wedges for extra zing.

Heat a wok over a high heat. Add the oil and swirl to coat. Add the onion and stir-fry for 1 minute or until tender. Add the tofu and stir-fry for 4 minutes, then stir in the paste. Stir-fry for 2 minutes or until fragrant. Add the vegetables and continue to move everything around the pan for another minute.

Add the noodles to the wok. Stir-fry the mixture for 1–2 minutes or until heated through. Top with the chopped peanuts and chilli flakes. Serve with a wedge of lime on the side.

Noodle Toastie

Serves 2

1 pack instant noodles (any flavour), cooked according to the packet instructions

4 slices thick white bread

1 tbsp butter, room temperature

1 tbsp ketchup

1 tsp French's mustard

1½ tbsp grated Cheddar

This one is dirty ... and one of my favourite flavour combos. Ketchup and French's mustard make me happy – hope they do you, too!

Preheat your grill (broiler), sandwich maker or waffle machine to medium heat.

Butter the bread on both sides, then top one side with ketchup, mustard, cheese and noodles. Cover with the other slice of bread, then toast until the filling turns gooey and the toast is golden, about 2–2½ minutes per side.

Noodle Pizzas

Serves 1 very hungry person or 2

Base:

2 packs instant noodles, cooked according to the packet instructions

1 medium egg, beaten

salt and freshly ground black pepper

2 tbsp extra-virgin olive oil

These pizzas are so much fun. Eat them straight from the oven, though there'll be no danger of them sticking around!

Mix the noodles and egg in a bowl. Season with salt and pepper.

Heat the olive oil in a 20 cm (8 in) frying pan (skillet) over a medium heat until shimmering. Add the noodle mixture and press with the bottom of a spatula into an even layer that completely covers the bottom of the pan. Reduce the heat to low. Cook for 20 minutes, or until soft, then remove from the pan and top with one of the suggested toppings below.

Ham & Pineapple

1 noodle pizza base (see above)

3 tbsp passata or tomato purée (paste)

50 g (2 oz) grated mozzarella

30 g (1 oz) shredded ham

30 g (1 oz) pineapple chunks

Preheat the oven to 180°C (350°F/Gas 4). Add the toppings to the pizza base and bake for 10 minutes. Remove from the pan, slide onto a plate, slice and eat.

Chorizo, Pesto & Mozzarella

1 noodle pizza base
(see p 71)

50 g (2 oz) grated
mozzarella

30 g (1 oz) chorizo,
chopped and cooked

1 tbsp green pesto

Preheat the oven to 180°C (350°F/Gas 4). Add the toppings to the pizza base and bake for 10 minutes. Remove from the pan, slide onto a plate, slice and eat.

Spinach, Chilli & Egg

1 noodle pizza base
(see p 71)

1 tbsp passata or sun-dried
tomato paste

handful of baby spinach

1 medium egg

1 red chilli, deseeded and
thinly sliced

20 g (¾ oz) feta (optional)

Preheat the oven to 180°C (350°F/Gas 4). Top the pizza with the passata or sun-dried tomato paste and spinach. Crack over the egg, sprinkle over the chilli and feta, if using. Bake for 10 minutes. Remove from the pan, slide onto a plate, slice and eat.

Margherita

1 noodle pizza base
(see p 71)

2 tbsp passata

1 tbsp sun-dried tomato
paste

pinch of oregano

60 g (2 oz) grated
mozzarella

10 g (½ oz) grated
Parmesan (optional)

handful of fresh basil
leaves

Preheat the oven to 180°C (350°F/Gas 4). Add the toppings to the pizza base and bake for 10 minutes. Remove from the pan, slide onto a plate, slice and eat.

Ramen Burger

Serves 2

Noodle buns:

200 g (7 oz) ramen noodles, cooked according to the packet instructions

1 medium egg, beaten

2 tbsp rapeseed oil

Burgers:

2 beef patties

salt and freshly ground black pepper

1 tbsp teriyaki sauce

2 tbsp sesame oil

2 slices Cheddar or Monterey Jack (optional)

2 tbsp mustard relish

2 tbsp wasabi mayonnaise

50 g (2 oz) Chinese cabbage, shredded

1 radish, thinly sliced

1 pinch chives

Sriracha, to serve

This spin on a traditional burger with the addition of Japanese flavours is sure to impress!

Let the noodles cool to room temperature. In a small mixing bowl, stir the egg into the noodles, tossing thoroughly to coat. Divide the egg-dressed noodles into 4 portions, and place each into a round 9 cm (3½ in) mould. Alternatively, if you do not have any moulds, shape the buns using your hands. They will be looser, but delicious all the same.

Add the oil to a frying pan (skillet) and set over a medium-high heat. Once the oil begins to shimmer, place the noodle buns into the pan in their moulds (if using) and use a small ramekin to press them down. Cook until the bottom is a dark golden brown. Flip both of the noodle buns, and cook until a dark golden brown on both sides, then carefully remove from the moulds.

Season the beef patties with salt, pepper, teriyaki sauce and sesame oil. Wipe out the frying pan and cook the patties over a medium-high heat for about 4 minutes on each side until medium rare, or to your preference. Top with a slice of cheese, if using.

Assemble the burgers, starting with the ramen bun, followed by the mustard relish, burger patty (cheese side up), wasabi mayonnaise, cabbage, radish, chives and Sriracha. Top with the other ramen noodle bun.

Note: For a quick wasabi mayonnaise, mix 1 teaspoon wasabi with 3 tablespoons mayonnaise.

Noodle Fry-up

Serves 2

2 × 100 g (3½ oz) packets instant chicken-flavour noodles, cooked according to the packet instructions

2 spring onions (scallions), thinly sliced

3 tbsp plain (all-purpose) flour

1 tbsp soy sauce (optional)

6 medium eggs

salt and freshly ground black pepper

vegetable oil, for frying

4 bacon rashers

30 g (1 oz) cherry tomatoes on the vine

200 g (7 oz) mushrooms

100 g (3½ oz) baked beans in sauce

Noodle patties give you a new way to soak up all the yummy fry-up juices.

Place the noodles in a large bowl. Allow to cool for 5 minutes. Add the spring onions, flour and soy sauce, if desired, to the noodles. Season with salt and pepper. Mix until well combined. Beat 2 of the eggs together. Stir into the noodle mixture.

Pour the oil into a 20 cm (8 in) frying pan (skillet) until 1 cm (½ in) deep. Heat over a medium heat. Using a ladle of mixture per noodle cake, drop 2 noodle cakes into the hot oil. Gently flatten with a spatula. Cook for 2–3 minutes on each side or until golden and cooked through. Transfer to a tray lined with paper towels to drain off any excess oil. Repeat with the remaining mixture, adding more oil if necessary.

Meanwhile, preheat the grill (broiler) to high. Place the bacon and cherry tomatoes on a tray lined with foil. Grill (broil) until the bacon is crisp and tomatoes have softened – keep an eye on this as bacon can go from crispy to burnt very quickly. Heat a 20 cm (8 in) frying pan over a medium heat and cook the mushrooms with a pinch of salt until soft. Set aside and keep warm. Next, heat ½ tablespoon oil in a pan, add the eggs, one at a time, and cook for 1–2 minutes on each side or until just set. Meanwhile heat up the baked beans in the microwave or in a saucepan on the hob and keep warm.

Place 2 noodle cakes on each serving plate and top with the remaining ingredients.

Butternut Noodle Pancake

~~~~~~~~~~~

Serves 2

150 g (5 oz) vermicelli rice noodles, cooked according to the packet instructions

150 g (5 oz) store-bought butternut spaghetti

4 medium eggs, whisked

1/2 tsp cinnamon or 1/2 tsp mixed spice

100 g (3 1/2 oz) self-raising flour

50 ml (2 fl oz) double (heavy) cream or yoghurt

1 tbsp caster (superfine) sugar

30 g (1 oz) butter

yoghurt, pecans and maple syrup, to serve

Spicy, warming and light all-in-one pancakes served with maple syrup, pecans and a dollop of yoghurt – what's not to like?

In a bowl, combine the vermicelli noodles, butternut spaghetti, eggs, cinnamon, flour, cream and sugar. Set aside for 30 minutes.

Add the butter to a 20 cm (8 in) frying pan (skillet) and heat for a few minutes. Then add 1 ladle of the noodle pancake mixture. Cook over a moderate heat for 2–2 1/2 minutes until golden brown on the underside. Flip over and cook for a further 2–2 1/2 minutes until set and cooked through. Repeat until you have 6 pancakes. Serve topped with a dollop of yoghurt, pecans and maple syrup.

PARTY

Lemongrass Larb

Serves 2-4

150 g (5 oz) dried rice vermicelli noodles, cooked according to the packet instructions

1 tbsp vegetable oil

1 tbsp ginger paste

2 tbsp lemongrass paste

2 garlic cloves, crushed

1 long red chilli, deseeded and chopped

400 g (14 oz) beef mince

2 tbsp honey

2 tbsp fish sauce

juice of 1 lemon

½ small bunch fresh mint, leaves picked

½ small bunch fresh coriander (cilantro), leaves picked

4 little gem lettuce, leaves separated

lime wedges, to serve

This dish is perfect for parties. Instead of beef, you could use chicken or turkey mince. Alternatively, as a vegetarian option, you could use mushrooms.

Heat the oil over a medium heat in a 20 cm (8 in) frying pan (skillet). Add the ginger, lemongrass, garlic and chilli and cook for 4-5 minutes or until fragrant.

Add the beef mince to the pan and increase the heat to high. Stir-fry, breaking up with a wooden spoon, for 5-6 minutes or until browned. Add the honey and fish sauce. Stir-fry for 4-5 minutes or until the beef mixture is golden and cooked. Stir in the lemon juice, mint and coriander.

Divide the beef mixture among the lettuce cups. Top with the noodles and serve with lime wedges.

Lime Dragon Noodles

Serves 2

200 g (7 oz) flat rice noodles, cooked according to the packet instructions

juice of 2 limes

1 tbsp Sriracha

2 tbsp soy sauce

1 tbsp honey

1 tbsp ginger paste

1 tbsp vegetable oil

250 g (9 oz) raw tiger prawns (shrimp)

2 medium eggs

2 spring onions (scallions), sliced diagonally

1 long red chilli, deseeded and halved lengthways (optional)

How to pimp in style. Zingy, limey noodles with prawns (shrimp) and scrambled eggs – all in one bowl.

In a bowl, mix the juice of 1 lime, the Sriracha, soy sauce, honey and ginger, and set aside. In a frying pan (skillet) over a high heat, fry the prawns with the oil and 1 tablespoon of the Sriracha mixture until cooked. Set aside.

Crack the eggs into a small bowl and whisk with a fork. Pour the egg into the pan and stir it well. Use a spatula to move the egg around quickly so it cooks in a scrambled style. After 2 minutes, or when the egg is cooked, take the pan off the heat. Add the remaining Sriracha mixture, the noodles and prawns. Squeeze over the other lime and serve with the spring onions scattered over the top and red chilli, if using.

Noodle Fritters with Satay Sauce

Makes 12–15 fritters

150 g (5 oz) rice vermicelli noodles, cooked according to the packet instructions

2 spring onions (scallions), thinly sliced

100 g (3½ oz) tinned sweetcorn

1 courgette (zucchini), coarsely grated

1 long red chilli, deseeded and finely chopped

2 tbsp soy sauce

1 tbsp oyster sauce

1 tsp sesame oil

100 g (3½ oz) self-raising flour

3 medium eggs, lightly beaten

2 tbsp vegetable oil

3 sprigs fresh mint, leaves picked, to serve

3 small cucumbers, halved, to serve

lime wedges, to serve

Satay sauce:

100 g (3½ oz) crunchy peanut butter

2 tbsp soy sauce

1 tbsp runny honey

1 tsp Sriracha

1 tbsp ginger paste

100 ml (3½ fl oz) water

squeeze of lime

This is such a moreish meal and the satay sauce is a quick way to pimp any dish.

Combine the spring onions, sweetcorn, courgette, chilli, soy sauce, oyster sauce, sesame oil and flour in a bowl. Add the eggs, stir to combine, then add the noodles.

Heat the oil in a 20 cm (8 in) frying pan (skillet) set over a medium-high heat. Using 1 tablespoon of the mixture at a time, cook in batches, for 2 minutes each side or until golden and cooked through. Transfer to a plate lined with paper towels. Cover with foil to keep warm or put in an oven preheated to 180°C (350°F/Gas 4) on a baking tray lined with foil.

Meanwhile, place all the satay sauce ingredients into a small saucepan, bring to the boil then turn off the heat. Serve the fritters with the satay sauce, mint, cucumbers and lime wedges.

Crispy Slaw

~~~~~~~~~~~~~~~~~~~~~~~

**Serves 2 as a main
or 4 as a side**

100 g (3½ oz) crunchy
noodles such as
supernoodles, cooked
according to the packet
instructions

½ Chinese cabbage or
white cabbage, thinly sliced

4 spring onions (scallions),
thinly sliced

1 medium carrot, peeled,
grated

100 g (3½ oz) beansprouts,
trimmed

100 g (3½ oz) mangetout
(snow peas), thinly sliced

2 tbsp chilli jam or sweet
chilli sauce

2 tbsp vegetable oil

juice of 2 limes

1 tbsp soy sauce

1 tsp sesame oil (optional)

½ small bunch fresh
coriander (cilantro) leaves,
chopped

salt and freshly ground
black pepper

drizzle of Maggi seasoning
(optional), to serve

Zingy, crispy, crunchy – a great crowd-pleasing salad.

To crisp the noodles, place them in the oven on a lined
baking tray for 20 minutes at 180°C (350°F/Gas 4) until
dried and crunchy. Set aside.

Place the cabbage, spring onions, carrot, beansprouts and
mangetout in a large bowl.

Combine the chilli jam or sauce, oil, lime juice, soy sauce
and sesame oil, if using, together in a bowl and add the
chopped coriander. Pour over the cabbage mixture. Season
with salt and pepper. Toss to combine. Sprinkle with the
noodles. Serve with a drizzle of Maggi seasoning, if using.

Bhuja-POP Mix

100 g (3½ oz) egg noodles, cooked according to the packet instructions, cooled and roughly chopped

1 tbsp rapeseed oil

60 g (2 oz) raisins

60 g (2 oz) roasted peanuts

Spice mix:

3 tbsp ghee

2 tsp black mustard seeds

2 tsp cumin seeds

2 tsp ground coriander

1 tsp garam masala

2 tsp tumeric

1 tsp curry leaves

1 tsp sea salt

large pinch of chilli flakes

Popcorn:

½ tbsp rapeseed oil

1 tbsp ghee

35 g (1 oz) popcorn kernels

½ tbsp curry powder

½ tsp chilli powder

pinch of salt

A great snack, treat or non-stop munch fest . . . that's all I'm saying.

Place the noodles in a 20 cm (8 in) frying pan (skillet) with 1 tablespoon oil and allow them to crisp up for about 15–20 minutes. Add the ghee, spices, curry leaves, salt and chilli flakes and allow them to infuse on a medium heat, making sure that they do not burn.

For the popcorn, heat the oil and ghee in a 3-litre (5¾-pint) saucepan with a tight-fitting lid over a medium-high heal until just before it smokes. Add the popcorn kernels, curry powder, chilli powder and salt immediately and reduce the heat a little. Swirl to cover the kernels with the oil, cover with the lid and cook, shaking the pan occasionally, for 1 minute 45 seconds or until the popping sounds have stopped. Take care at this stage not to burn the curry powder in the ghee – if it has reached smoking point it will become bitter and burnt.

Tip the popcorn into a large wide bowl and add the raisins and peanuts. When the spiced noodles are ready, tip them into the same bowl and mix well. Store in an airtight container for up to 2 weeks.

Quick Mushroom & Bacon Ragù

Serves 2

280 g (10 oz) egg noodles, cooked according to the packet instructions

1½ tbsp olive oil

200 g (7 oz) bacon, cut into 1 cm (½-in) pieces, or 200 g (7 oz) lardons

1 small onion, roughly chopped

1 garlic clove, crushed

500 g (1 lb 2 oz) mixed sliced mushrooms

salt and freshly ground black pepper

1 tbsp tomato paste (purée)

1½ tbsp sun-dried tomato paste

1 rosemary stalk, leaves picked and roughly chopped

200 ml (7 fl oz) vegetable stock

handful of fresh parsley, chopped

1 tsp red wine vinegar

100 g (3½ oz) spiralized courgette (zucchini) (optional)

shaved Parmesan, crème fraîche and sweet chilli sauce, to serve

This a quick way to make ragù with maximum flavour. The use of pre-sliced mushrooms and lardons all add to the convenience and speed.

Toss the noodles in ½ teaspoon oil to prevent them from sticking together.

Heat the remaining oil in a saucepan and cook the bacon over a medium heat, uncovered, stirring constantly, for about 5 minutes until crispy.

Add the onion and garlic and stir until golden – about 1 minute. Add the mushrooms and a small pinch of salt and pepper. Cover and cook until the juices have evaporated, stirring occasionally, about 20 minutes.

Stir in the tomato pastes, rosemary and stock until combined. Cover and cook until the sauce has thickened, 10–15 minutes.

Stir in the parsley and vinegar. Taste the ragù and see if it needs any more salt and pepper.

To serve, toss the noodles and courgette mix (if using) with the ragù. Finish with Parmesan, crème fraîche and sweet chilli sauce.

Quick
Prawn Laksa

Serves 2

1 tsp vegetable oil

1 garlic clove, crushed

1 spring onion (scallions), chopped

1 tbsp peeled and grated ginger

1 fresh green chilli, halved

juice of ½ lime

100 g (3½ oz) raw tiger prawns (shrimp)

200 ml (7 fl oz) coconut milk

150 ml (5 fl oz) vegetable stock

100 g (3 ½ oz) dried egg noodles

1 carrot, shredded

1 tbsp chopped fresh coriander (cilantro), to serve

lime wedges, to serve

Laksa paste:

2 fresh red chillies, deseeded if you like

2 garlic cloves, roughly chopped

4 cm (1½ in) piece ginger, peeled and roughly chopped

1 small onion, roughly chopped

1 stick lemongrass, outer layer discarded, roughly chopped

1 tbsp Thai fish sauce

The even quicker version of this is to use a pre-made laksa paste, but if you have the time, make the paste from scratch – it won't disappoint. The leftover paste can be stored in the fridge for two weeks in a sealed container.

If making the laksa paste from scratch, blitz all the ingredients together in a food processor until they form a paste.

Heat the oil in a large pan or wok. When hot, throw in the garlic, spring onion, ginger, chilli and 1 tablespoon laksa paste. Cook over a medium heat for 3–4 minutes, then add the lime juice.

Stir in the prawns, then add the coconut milk and stock. Simmer gently for 5 minutes over a low heat until the prawns are pink.

Meanwhile, cook the egg noodles in a pan of boiling water for 4 minutes until soft. Drain, then tip into the laksa pan. Season to taste, then serve in bowls, topped with the coriander and with lime wedges on the side.

Red Curry Noodle Bowl

~~~~~~~~

Serves 2

1 tbsp oil

2 spring onions (scallions), chopped

1 tbsp fresh ginger, peeled and sliced

2 tbsp red curry paste

200 ml (7 fl oz) coconut milk

200 ml (7 fl oz) chicken or vegetable stock

1 tbsp caster (superfine) sugar

1 tbsp hot chilli paste (sambal oelek)

2 tbsp fish sauce

1 tbsp soy sauce

1 bird's eye chilli, halved lengthways

2 kaffir lime leaves (optional)

60 g (2 oz) chopped broccoli florets, blanched

60 g (2 oz) spiralized courgette (zucchini)

handful of kale, blanched

60 g (2 oz) chopped asparagus, blanched

100 g (3½ oz) shredded cooked chicken, optional

100 g (3½ oz) brown rice noodles

1 lime, halved, to serve

handful of fresh coriander (cilantro), to serve

As well as being pretty, this is a lovely, hearty bowl, full of goodness.

Heat the oil in a large saucepan. Add the spring onions and ginger and stir-fry for 3–5 minutes. Add the curry paste and stir-fry for 1 minute. Add the coconut milk, stock, sugar, chilli paste, fish sauce, soy sauce, chilli and lime leaves, if using. Simmer for 15 minutes.

Add the vegetables and chicken (if using), then stir in the noodles until just combined (if you cook them for too long, the noodles will become too sticky). Serve topped with a squeeze of lime and the coriander leaves.

Bibimbap-style Noodle Bowl

Serves 2

100 g (3½ oz) black rice noodles, cooked according to the packet instructions

2 fried eggs (see p 25)

5 cm (2 in) piece ginger, peeled and finely grated

1 garlic clove, finely chopped

2 tbsp soy sauce

100 g (3½ oz) firm tofu, cut into 1 cm (½ in) slices

1 tbsp sesame seeds

2 tbsp vegetable oil

200 g (7 oz) green beans, trimmed, halved

100 g (3½ oz) mushrooms, sliced

1 large carrot, cut into thin matchsticks

salt and freshly ground black pepper

50 g (2 oz) red cabbage, finely shredded

2 spring onions (scallions), thinly sliced diagonally

Dressing:

2 tbsp white wine vinegar

3 tsp sambal oelek or hot chilli sauce

pinch of caster (superfine) sugar

1 tsp sesame oil

This is the perfect marriage of fresh ingredients, spices and full-on flavour – nourishing and delicious. Bibimbap is a Korean dish meaning 'mixed rice' – but it's just as delicious with noodles!

Combine the ginger, garlic and soy sauce in a bowl. Add the tofu and stir until well coated in the marinade, then set aside for 10 minutes.

Place the sesame seeds on a plate. Transfer the tofu to a separate plate, reserving the marinade. Press one side of the tofu slices into the sesame seeds to coat them. Return the tofu to the plate.

Heat 1 tablespoon oil in a 20 cm (8 in) frying pan (skillet) over a high heat. Add the beans, mushrooms and carrot, and stir-fry, making sure that the vegetables are semi-charred. Season with salt and pepper, then set aside.

Heat the remaining oil in a 20 cm (8 in) pan. Add the tofu, sesame-side down. Cook for 2 minutes or until the seeds are golden. Turn and cook for a further 2–3 minutes or until heated through.

To make the dressing, whisk the ingredients together with 2 teaspoons water in a small jug.

Arrange the noodles, stir-fried vegetables, tofu, cabbage and spring onions in 2 serving bowls. Season with salt and black pepper. Top with the fried eggs. Drizzle with the dressing and serve with the reserved tofu marinade.

Sweet Kugels

Makes 12 (muffin size) cakes

180 g (6 oz) medium egg noodles, cooked according to the packet instructions and cooled

60 g (2 oz) raisins

60 g (2 oz) flaked almonds

4 medium eggs, whisked

120 g (4 oz) sour cream

250 g (9 oz) cottage cheese

100 g (3½ oz) cream cheese

100 g (3½ oz) caster (superfine) sugar, plus a little extra for dusting

60 g (2 oz) butter, melted

cinnamon and icing (confectioner's) sugar for dusting

This recipe is a take on the Jewish baked pudding, which uses noodles in a sweet setting.

Preheat the oven to 180°C (350°F/Gas 4). Line a 12-hole muffin tin with muffin cases.

Place the raisins, flaked almonds and noodles in a bowl. Add the eggs, sour cream, cottage cheese, cream cheese, sugar and butter. Mix well and pour evenly between the muffin cases. Top with a sprinkle of cinnamon and icing sugar, then bake for 40 minutes until set and golden. Check after 20 minutes – if they look like they are golden enough, reduce the oven temperature to 160°C (320°F/Gas 3) for the next 20 mins. Once cooled, keep in the fridge for up to 1 week.

Nutella®
Swirl Pots

~~~~~~~~~~

Serves 3-4

Crispy spider noodles:

100 g (3½ oz) vermicelli rice noodles, cooked according to the packet instructions

2 tbsp caster (superfine) sugar

½ tbsp cocoa powder

Nutella® swirl cheesecake:

250 g (9 oz) cream cheese, room temperature

80 g (3 oz) icing (confectioner's) sugar, sifted

100 g (3½ oz) Nutella®

So simple to make and fun to serve.

For the crispy noodles, preheat the oven to 180°C (350°F/Gas 4) and line a tray with baking parchment. In a bowl, mix the noodles and sugar, then place on the baking tray. Sprinkle over the cocoa powder and bake in the oven until crispy – approx 30 minutes. Remove from the oven, allow to cool and break up the noodles. Place in an airtight container for up to 2 weeks.

For the cheesecake mixture, use a wooden spoon to beat together the cream cheese and sifted icing sugar in a bowl, until you have a creamy mixture. Stir in the Nutella®, but do not overmix as you want to keep it swirly. Spoon into 4 glasses and allow to set in the fridge for 1 hour minimum. Serve with 2 tablespoons crispy spider noodles per glass.

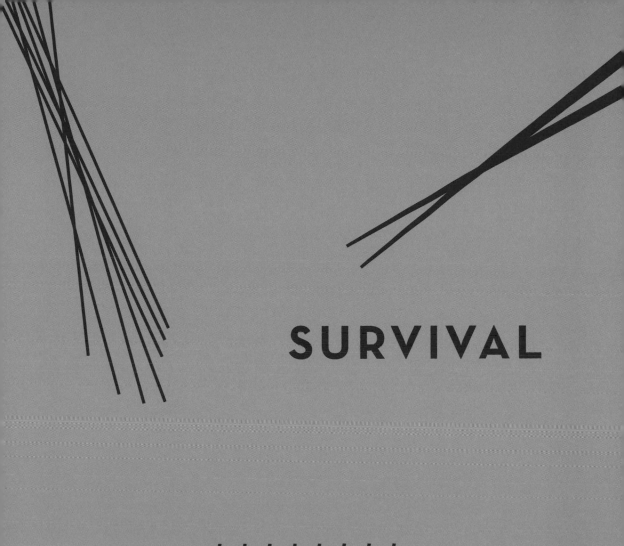

SURVIVAL

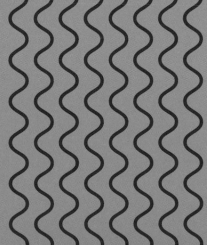

Mugestroni

Serves 1

1 mug vegetable juice (like V8) or tinned tomato soup

40 g (1½ oz) tinned borlotti beans

60 g (2 oz) frozen vegetables

15–20 g (½–¾ oz) vermicelli noodles

fresh parsley, to serve (optional)

½ tbsp Parmesan shavings, to serve (optional)

pinch of chilli flakes, to serve (optional)

pesto, to serve (optional)

A perfect duvet-day treat – serve with crusty bread.

Pour the juice or soup into a mug and add the borlotti beans, vegetables and noodles, then heat in the microwave on high for 2–3 minutes. Alternatively, bring the mixture to the boil in a saucepan on the hob. You want to heat it up enough to cook the noodles and frozen veg thoroughly – this takes around 4 minutes.

Serve topped with the parsley, Parmesan, chilli flakes and pesto, if using.

Noodle Chorizo Frittata

Serves 2

70 g (2½ oz) egg noodles, cooked according to the packet instructions

1 tbsp olive oil

120 g (4 oz) chorizo, chopped

2 tbsp sun-dried tomato paste

100 g (3½ oz) spinach

5 medium eggs, beaten

salt and freshly ground black pepper

3 spring onions (scallions), chopped

2–3 tbsp crème fraîche (optional)

handful of fresh parsley, chopped

Spicy chorizo and fresh spring onions (scallions) combine in this delicious frittata.

Preheat the oven to 180°C (350°F/Gas 4).

Heat half the oil in an ovenproof frying pan over a medium-high heat and cook the chorizo for 10 minutes. Then add 1 tablespoon tomato paste and cook for another minute. Combine the chorizo with the noodles in a bowl. Add the remaining oil to the pan, then cook the spinach until wilted.

Season the beaten eggs with salt and black pepper, then add them to the pan along with the cooked noodles and chorizo mix and the spring onions. Cook without stirring for 3–4 minutes. Dollop over the crème fraîche (if using) and the reserved tomato paste. Transfer to the oven and cook for a further 5 minutes, or until the top is set. Sprinkle the parsley over the top of the cooked frittata and serve straight from the pan.

Noodle, Ham, Corn & Cheese Loaf

Makes 8 portions

150 g (5 oz) rice vermicelli noodles, cooked according to the packet instructions

½ tbsp olive oil, plus a little extra for greasing

1 small onion, finely chopped

100 g (3½ oz) bacon, chopped, or lardons

1 garlic clove, crushed

1 small courgette (zucchini), grated

100 g (3½ oz) sweetcorn kernels

60 g (2 oz) Cheddar, grated

60 g (2 oz) self-raising flour

5 medium eggs, lightly beaten

handful of fresh chives, finely chopped

Eat a slice of this just out of the oven. Or, serve it toasted with melted cheese and drizzled with hot chilli sauce.

Preheat the oven 180°C (350°F/Gas 4). Grease a 900 g (2 lb) loaf tin and line it with baking parchment.

Heat the oil in a 20 cm (8 in) frying pan (skillet), and sauté the onion and bacon for 5 minutes. Then add the garlic, frying for another minute.

Meanwhile mix the courgette, sweetcorn, Cheddar, flour, eggs, chives and noodles in a bowl.

Add the onion and bacon mixture and mix in well. Pour into the prepared loaf tin and bake for 45 minutes. Test whether the loaf is done by inserting a skewer – if it comes out clean, the loaf is done. Remove from the oven and allow to cool.

The loaf keeps, refrigerated, for up to 1 week.

Prosciutto, Mozzarella & Tomato Noodle Bake

Serves 2

150 g (5 oz) thin egg noodles, cooked according to the packet instructions

1 tbsp olive oil, plus extra for greasing

1 × 400 g (14 oz) tin chopped tomatoes

2 garlic cloves, peeled and crushed

1 tbsp sun-dried tomato paste

½ small bunch fresh basil, leaves picked

salt and freshly ground black pepper

½ tsp caster (superfine) sugar

125 g (4 oz) mozzarella ball, torn

60 g (2 oz) Cheddar, grated

90 g (3 oz) prosciutto, torn

An Italian-style bake which is as good eaten cold as it is served hot.

Preheat the oven to 180°C (350°F/Gas 4). Grease a 25 cm (10 in) baking dish with olive oil.

Heat the oil in a saucepan, and add the chopped tomatoes, garlic, tomato paste and a couple of the basil leaves and cook for 10 minutes. Season with salt and pepper. Combine the noodles with the tomato sauce and sugar, then pour into the baking dish with the noodles. Top with the mozzarella, Cheddar, prosciutto and the remaining basil leaves.

Bake for 40 minutes until bubbling and golden. Leave to cool slightly before serving.

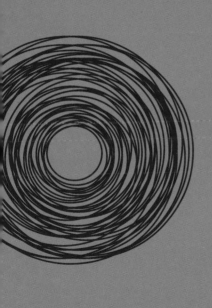

ONE POT

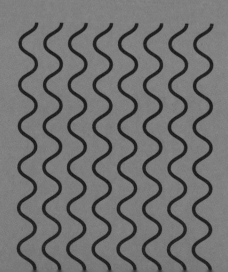

Butter
& Lemon

〜〜〜

Serves 1

100 g (3½ oz) instant
noodles, cooked according
to the packet instructions,
drained and 2 tbsp water
reserved

1½ tbsp butter

juice and grated zest of
1 lemon

handful of Cheddar or
Parmesan (optional)

cracked black pepper

These noodles are a creamy citrus sensation.

Add the reserved noodle water, butter, lemon juice and
zest to a saucepan and heat up, mixing well to blend. Turn
up the heat and add the noodles and cheese, if using, and a
good amount of cracked pepper. By this time, the noodles
may need another ½ tablespoon water as they continue to
absorb the sauce. Take off the heat, grab a fork and eat.

Parmesan Cream
& Black Pepper

〜〜〜

Serves 1

100 g (3½ oz) instant
noodles, cooked according
to the packet instructions,
drained and 2 tbsp water
reserved

60 g (2 oz) double (heavy)
cream

1 garlic clove, crushed

2 tbsp grated Parmesan

1 tsp cracked black pepper

Sometimes the simplest flavours are the most effective.

Add the reserved noodle water and cream to a saucepan
and heat up, mixing well to blend. Turn up the heat and
add the noodles for 1 minute. Take off the heat, then add
the garlic, Parmesan and pepper. By this time, the noodles
may need another ½ tablespoon water as they continue to
absorb the sauce. Grab a fork and eat.

Rosie's Dirty Noodles

~~~~~~~~

Serves 1

100 g (3½ oz) instant noodles, cooked according to the packet instructions, drained and 2 tbsp water reserved

1 tbsp miso paste

1 tbsp black bean chilli paste

Deliciously dirty.

Add the reserved noodle water, miso paste and black bean chilli paste to a saucepan and heat up, mixing well to blend. Turn up the heat and add the noodles. Take off the heat. By this time, the noodles may need another ½ tablespoon water as they continue to absorb the sauce. Grab a fork and eat.

Kimchi & Parmesan

~~~~~~~~

Serves 1

100 g (3½ oz) instant noodles, cooked according to the packet instructions, drained and 2 tbsp water reserved

60 g (2 oz) kimchi

generous pinch of Parmesan (optional)

Korean and Italian flavours are combined in one pot.

Add the reserved noodle water and kimchi to a saucepan and heat up, mixing well to blend. Turn up the heat and add the noodles. Take off the heat and add the Parmesan, if using. By this time, the noodles may need another ½ tablespoon water as they continue to absorb the sauce. Grab a fork and eat.

Tahini
& Onion

~~~~~~~~~

Serves 1

100 g (3½ oz) instant noodles, cooked according to the packet instructions, drained and 2 tbsp water reserved

1 tbsp tahini

1 tbsp extra virgin olive oil

squeeze of lemon juice

2 spring onions (scallions), sliced

1 tsp mixed sesame seeds

handful of grated Parmesan

pinch of chilli flakes

lemon zest (optional)

Nutty, creamy, oh-so-dreamy.

Add the reserved noodle water, tahini, olive oil and lemon juice to a saucepan and heat up, mixing well to blend. Turn up the heat and add the noodles, spring onions, sesame seeds, Parmesan and chilli flakes. By this time, the noodles may need another ½ tablespoon water as they continue to absorb the sauce. Take off the heat, grab a fork and eat.

Marmite®
Avo

~~~~~~~~~

Serves 1

100 g (3½ oz) instant noodles, cooked according to the packet instructions, drained and 2 tbsp water reserved

1 tbsp butter

1–2 tsp Marmite® or Vegemite®, or to taste

½ avocado, scooped and cut into quarters

handful of grated Cheddar

Love it or hate it, these noodles are guaranteed to cause a stir.

Add the reserved noodle water, butter and Marmite® or Vegemite® to a saucepan and heat up, mixing well to blend. Turn up the heat and add the noodles, avocado and Cheddar. By this time, the noodles may need another ½ tablespoon water as they continue to absorb the sauce. Take off the heat, grab a fork and eat.

Hazelnut Nutella®

Serves 1

100 g (3½ oz) instant noodles, cooked according to the packet instructions, drained and 2 tbsp water reserved

2 tbsp Nutella®

1 tbsp chopped hazelnuts

It might sounds nuts, but this is totally tasty.

Add the reserved noodle water and Nutella® to a saucepan and heat up, mixing well to blend. Turn up the heat and add the noodles. By this time, the noodles may need another ½ tablespoon water as they continue to absorb the sauce. Take off the heat, add the hazelnuts, grab a fork and eat.

Raspberry & Peanut Butter

Serves 1

100 g (3½ oz) instant noodles, cooked according to the packet instructions, drained and 2 tbsp water reserved

2 tbsp peanut butter

handful of raspberries

This classic flavour combo is extra sweet with noodles.

Add the reserved noodle water and peanut butter to a saucepan and heat up, mixing well to blend. Turn up the heat and add the noodles. By this time, the noodles may need another ½ tablespoon water as they continue to absorb the sauce. Take off the heat, add the raspberries, grab a fork and eat.

Lime & Coconut

Serves 1

100 g (3½ oz) instant noodles, cooked according to the packet instructions, drained and 2 tbsp water reserved

60 ml (2 fl oz) coconut milk

juice and grated zest of 1 lime

1 tbsp desiccated coconut

Give your noodles a tropical twist.

Add the reserved noodle water, the coconut milk, lime juice and zest to a saucepan and heat up, mixing well to blend. Turn up the heat and add the noodles. By this time, the noodles may need another ½ tablespoon water as they continue to absorb the sauce. Take off the heat, add the coconut, grab a fork and eat.

Cinnamon & Orange

Serves 1

100 g (3½ oz) instant noodles, cooked according to the packet instructions drained and 2 tbsp water reserved

60 ml (2 fl oz) condensed milk

zest of ½ orange or 1 tbsp marmalade

pinch of ground cinnamon (optional)

The hit of cinnamon gives this one-pot wonder a comforting warmth.

Add the reserved noodle water and condensed milk to a saucepan and heat up, mixing well to blend. Turn up the heat and add the noodles. By this time, the noodles may need another ½ tablespoon water as they continue to absorb the sauce. Take off the heat, add the orange zest and cinnamon, if using, grab a fork and eat.

Ten-Minute Ramen

~~~~~~~~~~

Serves 2

200 g (7 oz) ramen noodles, cooked according to the packet instructions

2 × 7-minute eggs (see p 26), or soy eggs (see p 28), peeled and halved

200 g (7 oz) sliced cooked pork (thinly sliced pork neck works best here)

100 g (3½ oz) mixed greens (kale, pak choy and spinach)

1 sheet sliced nori seaweed paper, to serve

sprinkle of sesame seeds, to serve

2 spring onions (scallions), thinly sliced, to serve

Broth:

500 ml (17 fl oz) chicken stock

2 garlic cloves, peeled and bruised

2 tbsp soy sauce

1 tsp Worcestershire sauce

½ tsp Chinese five spice

dash of chilli powder

1 tsp caster (superfine) sugar

2 slices of fresh ginger, peeled

Goodness in a bowl for body and soul. If desired, serve with your own kecap manis (Indonesian sweet soy sauce), made by stirring together 1 tablespoon soy sauce, ½ tablespoon honey and a splash of mirin.

Add all of the broth ingredients to a stockpot or large saucepan and bring to the boil. Reduce the heat and simmer for 5 minutes.

Divide the noodles between 2 soup bowls. Arrange the pork on top of the noodles, along with the greens and eggs.

Bring the stock to the boil once again, then take it off the heat and divide it among the soup bowls.

Allow the greens to slightly wilt before serving topped with nori, sesame seeds and spring onions. If you wish, pimp with kecap manis (see above).

Note: If you're not using store-bought cooked pork, try this simple recipe. Preheat the oven to 180°C (350°F/Gas 4). Place 200 g (7 oz) pork neck on a baking tray with a drizzle of oil, soy sauce & kecap manis (see above) until cooked through.

Noodle & Sweet Potato Rösti

Serves 2

100 g (3½ oz) egg noodles, cooked according to the packet instructions and cooled

2 tbsp olive oil

2 sweet potatoes, scrubbed and coarsely grated

salt and freshly ground black pepper

handful of rocket (arugula)

50 g (2 oz) crumbled goat's cheese

sweet chilli sauce, to serve

A new take on the classic rösti. Traditionally, these are made with white potatoes, but substituting sweet potatoes makes them feel lighter. Finish with some sweet chilli sauce for an extra kick.

Heat 1 tablespoon oil over a medium to low heat in a 25 cm (10 in) frying pan (skillet). Place the grated sweet potatoes in a clean kitchen towel and squeeze out as much liquid as possible. In a bowl, mix the sweet potatoes with the noodles.

Add the sweet potatoes and noodles to the hot pan, pressing down on them with a spatula to form a flat surface. Cook for 12–15 minutes until the bottom of the cake is golden and crisp. Place a plate that is small enough to fit into the pan over the top of the potato rösti and invert the rösti onto the plate. Add the remaining oil to the hot pan and slide the rösti back in.

Continue to cook for 10–12 minutes until the rösti are golden on the other side. Reduce the heat to low and cook for another 2 minutes to crisp up the rösti. Season generously with salt and pepper, top with the rocket and goat's cheese, cut into wedges and serve. Add some sweet chilli sauce for an extra kick.

Quick Singapore Noodles

Serves 1

1 pack instant noodles, cooked according to the packet instructions

1 tbsp rapeseed oil

1 tsp curry powder

100 g (3½ oz) frozen vegetables

2 spring onions (scallions), chopped

a drizzle of soy sauce

hot chilli sauce (optional)

The combination of curry powder and noodles transports me to the streets of Singapore.

Heat the oil in a large 20 cm (8 in) frying pan (skillet) over a medium heat. Add the curry powder and cook for 30 seconds. Then add the frozen vegetables and spring onions, and cook for 2–3 minutes. Add the vegetable mixture to the cooked noodles and toss to combine. Add the soy sauce and chilli sauce, if using.

Greens with Oyster Sauce

2 tbsp oyster sauce

1 tbsp soy sauce

1 garlic clove, sliced

5 cm (2 in) piece of ginger, peeled and finely sliced

300 g (10½ oz) pak choi (bok choy)

An Asian staple, which makes a great side to any noodle dish. You can replace the pak choi with any green veg.

Place the oyster sauce, soy sauce, garlic and ginger into a bowl and stir well. Place the pak choi in a large pan of simmering water. Cook, uncovered, for 2–3 minutes or until tender. Pour the sauce mixture over the pak choi, toss and serve.

About the Author

Kathy Kordalis is a London-based food stylist and recipe writer. She has worked in the food industry for years and her experience includes managing the Divertimenti Cookery School and training as a chef at the Leiths School of Food and Wine. Her approach to food is light, relaxed and accessible, drawing inspiration from her classical training in London, along with her Australian and Mediterranean heritage. It's all about sharing with friends and family, and coming up with new recipes to excite them!

Acknowledgements

Thank you to the ever fabulous Kate Pollard and the great team at Hardie Grant. It is always such a pleasure to work with you. To Nicky Barneby for the design and to Delphine Phin for your hard work editing this book. Sarah Fassnidge for tasting and testing all the pimping noodles. To my shoot assistants Sarah Fassnidge and Stella Grant for your help and good humour. The super-talented Jacqui Melville for bringing this book to life with props and photography – I'm so grateful. Biggest thanks to Matthew and my family and friends the world over.

Index

Pimp My Noodles by Kathy Kordalis

First published in 2017 by Hardie Grant Books

Hardie Grant Books (UK)
52–54 Southwark Street
London SE1 1UN
hardiegrant.co.uk

Hardie Grant Books (Australia)
Ground Floor, Building 1
658 Church Street
Melbourne, VIC 3121
hardiegrant.com.au

British Library Cataloguing-in-Publication Data. A catalogue
record for this book is available from the British Library.

ISBN: 978-1-78488-123-8

Publisher: Kate Pollard
Senior Editor: Kajal Mistry
Editorial Assistant: Hannah Roberts
Publishing Assistant: Eila Purvis
Photographer: Jacqui Melville
Styling on pages 4, 14, 17, 18, 21, 24, 26, 27, 30, 31 and 137: Lucy Cufflin
Art Direction: Nicky Barneby
Copy editor: Delphine Phin
Proofreader: Charlotte Coleman-Smith
Indexer: Cathy Heath

Colour Reproduction by p2d
Printed and bound in China by 1010

10 9 8 7 6 5 4 3 2 1